Financial Mistakes

Financial Mistakes

instafool

Presents

Financial Mistakes

13 Biggest Common Money Mistakes to Avoid from Going Broke and to Start Building Wealth

Instafo

instafo

ISBN 978-1-708-15456-1

Printed in the United States of America

First Edition

FOOL'S GUIDE

Financial Mistakes

PROLOGUE:
The Fool Card

"A fool thinks himself to be wise, but a wise man knows himself to be a fool." – **William Shakespeare**

Ready to have your fortune read? Then pick a card...any card. Ah, congratulations! You have selected the **Fool card.** *Don't* *despair!* It is the most powerful one, being the omnipotent wild card as well as the first card in a tarot deck with the number 0, that represents new journey and new solution available with unlimited optimism, unexhausted enthusiasm, and undiscovered opportunities, because to a fool...anything is possible!

Yet, the fool is "nobody's fool" but is *secretly* the wisest of all, able to pull strings in the most dire situations due to a sharp wit, astute acumen, erudite knowledge, diligent resourcefulness, and perceptive observation of the world and what goes on around. Indeed cunning, evasive, and elusive to get ahead without being ensnared by the same established rules others played by, the fool is able to think and see things outside of the box.

With that said, you can learn a lot from the fool through all their intentional and unintentional antics.

Nobody likes to hear the truth. *The truth hurts...but is honest.* Historically, only the fool was sly enough to get away with the most unfavorable truth in the royal court from knowing everything that went on, without getting his own head chopped and served on a king's silver platter for the hidden genius disguised as superficial foolishness. Perhaps a forgivable trickster in this regard, the fool was, nonetheless and above all, a true survival of the fittest and a formidable force to behold.

If you want to possess the great wisdom of the fool in a modern era of instant information, look no further because you have found your tarot calling card: **Instafool.**

Being an Instafool is for those fools who dare question and go up against conventional knowledge, by exploring the polar opposite side of the coin which nobody else is willing do and by exposing the cold-hard truth which nobody else is willing to admit, in order to gain better perspective, bigger picture, and wider spectrum covering all aspects of everything in any area.

While the fool may be a joker, the Instafool is no joke or laughing matter. Being the Instafool is about being a renaissance visionary trailblazing innovative ideas and being an inquisitive intellect uncovering controversial truths and unapologetically and shamelessly willing to educate those truths, even when gaining ridicules from others.

It's better to be an Instafool than be fooled in a world full of so much instant MISinformation. *Know thy truth by knowing thy untruth.* That's the key role of the Instafool.

This now sums up the Instafool and your tarot card reading. What shall you do now is entirely up to you...

Shall you be audacious enough to follow this path of an Instafool?

ANECDOTE:
The Fool Iffy

Meet "Iffy the Fool" of the high king. He's the fool for the royal court's amusement by entertaining them, but more importantly...indirectly educating them with his endless clumsy antics at the expense of his competence and confidence...for all to see what not do and avoid.

Don't be like Iffy the Fool. Be the opposite of him through learning from his mistakes and doing the opposite of what he does.

Whether intentional or unintentional, the wise fool in disguised accidentally becomes the best teacher around.

He shall now be your guide...

F(OOL) ACT AT PLAY:
Burnt-Holes in Broke Pockets

Why do so many people have a hard time effectively managing their money today? *Are you one of them?*

It's easy to blame *that* on modern society. People just seem to organize their lives differently now. And with all the new habits of consumerism, we seem to have lost the financial accountabilities that our grandparents (and their parents) used to have.

In a way, the term "legacy" has lost its tangible value over time. Being able to leave a legacy to your children and the generations after them tends to be more skewed toward familial heritage or culture. But times have changed.

On the surface, it seems like only financially well-off people who have had successful careers and lives are able to teach their kids the nitty-gritty of solid financial sense. To the rest, these things may seem trivial because many believe that people will automatically pick them up eventually, for example, not teaching every student in school how to properly file taxes, which everybody will have to do, for Uncle Sam to collect his happy paycheck.

To be honest, there's nothing wrong with figuring things out for yourself. But here's the problem: When you don't get the basic knowledge about certain things, you end up making more mistakes and wasting more time than if you had learned them when you were young.

That's the problem with the majority of folks (particularly *"millennials"*) when it comes to important things—most notably **money**. And since money is a huge part of what it takes to make someone happy (and we are not talking about being rich but having a decent and comfortable life), it is important to know how to handle it, and, at least, not feel like you're always only making ends meet or you've worked your entire life for nothing, once you reach a certain age.

As a brief filter for now, here's what leads many people down the path toward their money mistakes:

- **Convenience.** Modern technology makes it ridiculously easy to be lazy. You can do just about anything by clicking "OK" or "Submit" on your smartphone or computer. You don't even have to get out of bed. Sure, this is convenient and can save time and effort, but there's still a price to pay in terms of service fees, shipping and handling costs, and other tradeoffs for such convenience.

- **Laziness.** People would rather take advantage of social programs set up by the government for a little help from time to time (sometimes too often). This one is inevitable, as some people would rather not take the proper steps into "stretching" their hard-earned dollars for a certain period and maybe look for other alternatives (like an additional job, going back to school or being able to earn more money, etc.) to maybe make things easier on themselves.

- **Impulse.** There are so many tempting options that we often choose without thinking twice about how it could hurt our bottom line, like fast food, transportation, online shopping, etc. People would rather opt for the quick solutions, forgetting that they are costly in the end. For example, if you choose to get a cab to drive somewhere that is only 10 minutes away when you could have walked. Think about this: If you were spending $50 a month just in taxi fare, you could have saved $600 in a year just by walking.

- **Acceptance.** The relationship we have with money is not shaped by how we are brought up but mostly by pop culture and the aggressive marketing techniques that are used. We sometimes feel pressured to follow trends so that we can appear cool and accepted by others, just to find out that these trends don't really help us but are just ways to drain more money out of our pockets.

- **Trend.** Newer trends make it difficult for this fast-paced generation to really stick to their financial priorities. For example, if getting some pricey plastic surgery done to have the perfect body were the hot new trend, many would go in debt just to achieve that.

Not knowing how to budget or not having the right spending reflexes is almost like walking into a very dark and hostile forest at night without a map or a flashlight. The map is like a great personal financial plan that you can follow or adjusts as you age and grow financially. And the flashlight is like all the little reflexes that you've learned to use after getting to know how to handle your money every day.

<u>SELF-EVALUATION</u>: Before we introduce our first money mistake, try this little self-evaluation as a warmup. Answer the following questions with *"Yes"* or *"No."*

1. Do you consistently find yourself barely having enough money to make it toward the end of a month?

2. Do you sometimes find yourself borrowing money just because you neglected an important bill?

3. Do you dine out more than you eat at home just because you don't feel like cooking?

4. Do you hate walking even though you know that sometimes you don't have much of a choice?

5. Do you dig into your savings or money intended to be used for something else for unexpected whim purchases?

6. Do you see words like "personal financial plan" as a scary notion that you will never be able to handle?

- If you've answered *"Yes"* to all or most of these questions, then you are making basic but very costly mistakes that are killing your chances to have a better quality of life through better personal financial management.

- If you've answered *"Yes"* to a couple of the questions, then you might be making a few mistakes because you like following trends, but you seem to be someone who also wants to improve their financial situation and is on the way to doing so.

- If you've answered *"No"* to all the questions or most of them, then you are a very responsible person when it comes to handling your money. Kudos! You have goals and ambitions and know just what to do when it comes to your finances and not wandering off the right track. Whatever your answer was, continue on to learn more about the various mistakes people make when it comes to money.

MISTAKE #1:
Frequent Eating Out

Eating out can make life easier, especially if you work all day and don't have the time or energy to cook when you get home. If your life revolves around work, you probably won't see the economic benefit of buying your own food to cook meals at home rather than dining out daily.

According to the Bureau of Labor Statistics, the average American household spends an average of $3,008 per year dining out. On top of that, the money spent on food "away from home" versus "at home" has risen 94% since the year 2003.

The culprit? Like we said earlier, this is largely attributed to our desire for ease and speed in getting things done (online ordering, restaurant chains all over, etc.). And for all you coffee snobs out there, don't think your daily cup of joe at Starbucks is exempt from this.

Extremely popular among millennials are food-service-delivery apps like Grubhub and Seamless (which are both virtually the same things owned by Grubhub Inc.) as well as Uber Eats, DoorDash, Postmates, among many others popping up now and then. For users, ordering through these apps seems convenient (and cool and hip) enough; but for restaurants, there is an associated fee to be listed on these apps, and to help offset that—the users tend to be presented with a higher-priced menu (on top of whatever other fees) than if they ordered in person or simply by phone. Even when choosing delivery through phoning, it's still typically cheaper than having it delivered through these food delivery apps because these apps have to make their money somehow to stay in operation. *(Remember: There ain't no such thing as a free lunch.)*

<u>REASONS</u>: You might not realize it at first, but when you add up all the meals you eat every day in a year, the difference between what you could have saved by cooking your own meals is nothing to sneeze at.

For example, if you spend on average $10 a day for three meals every month, you will spend $10 x 7 days x 4 weeks x 12 months = $3,360 per year just to eat out!

On the other hand, if you spend $100 every three months for pantry items (like rice, cooking oil, cereals, noodles, etc.), $20 every two months for meats, and $10 for perishables every two weeks, you'll end up spending ($100 x 4 times a year) + ($20 x 6 times a year) + ($20 x 12 months) = $760 every year for cooking at home.

The discrepancy is huge with $3,360 - $760 = $2,600 wasted on eating out.

<u>BENCHMARK</u>: Shop at least twice a month on a budget. Evaluate what you can afford when it comes to groceries

and try to buy only essential foods. So, what you will need is to:

1. Make a list of groceries with the food you'll need during the month like:

- Meats (chicken, pork, beef, fish, etc.)

- Fruits and vegetables (Keep it simple and stick to three to five types of fruits and veggies that you really like, such as five fruits like bananas, oranges, apples, grapes, strawberries. And for vegetables, a few green peppers, onions, garlic, eggplant, and tomatoes.)

- Starchy food (potatoes, rice, pasta, bread)

- Dairy (milk, cheese, yogurt, etc.)

- And other items, which could consist of cooking oils, a few snacks, drinks like sodas or fruit juices, spices, and others. Stick to five essential items that you really need, to make it simple.

2. Next, calculate how much you would need to afford all the items on your list.

3. Make sure to add $20 on top of what you calculated in step two, just in case your evaluation is off (like perhaps ending up being a few dollars short at the store). For instance, if your budget is $150 for all your food, then you should maximize your budget by adding $20 in case your list ends up costing more. (Of course, this is only an approximation for the first time you work with your list and given budget. Once you start using the same list every month, you'll know exactly how much you'll need.)

4. Your next step is to learn how to cook your own meals. The goal would be to actually cook a considerable amount of food in your free time (possibly on Sunday or whatever day you don't have work) and

store and freeze your meals in plastic containers so that all you need to do is just warm them up during the week. The principle is quite simple:

- For taste, fry some chopped onions mixed with garlic and spices. Add water regularly so they don't burn.

- When cooked, add about 1/2 a cup of water and then your beef or chicken and chopped vegetables, for a stew. Add salt and pepper at the end.

- When you want to bake chicken or meat, spread some mustard, salt, or spices on top. Or you can add some honey or maple syrup. Next, add your chopped onions (half an onion and garlic) on top and a small amount (1/4 a cup) of cooking oils (you have the choice between vegetable oils, coconut oil, or butter). Add a bit of water, then bake for 25 to 30 minutes until done.

- Side dishes like rice or boiled vegetables are easy to make. You can also learn to make your own gravy to enjoy your baked meats and side dishes.

- Baked meats stay good for two or three days in the fridge. You can also freeze some of your stew for longer-term storage while keeping the rest in the fridge to eat within a couple of days.

5. After you learn the basics of cooking, you should make your newly acquired skill more functional by doing the following:

- Cook two or three dishes that can make up five or six meals that will last several days.

- If you cook on a Sunday, keep the meal you will eat on Monday in the fridge, and freeze the remaining meals for the rest of the week.

- To save some time, before you leave your house for work, take a frozen meal out in the morning and move it to the fridge. This will allow you to simply warm it up when you get home later that day.

BENEFITS: You simply can't go wrong with doing your very own home cooking. You will save money and resources, and perhaps you can add one more activity to your financial plan, such as monthly savings.

TASK: Make up a new budget for your meals by opting to buy groceries instead of eating out. Apply these few methods: Make a list, create a budget for the list, learn the basics of cooking, then make eating at home more functional by learning how to preserve your meals for a whole week (such as storing in the fridge or freezer depending on when you plan to eat each meal).

MISTAKE #2:
Not Prioritizing Savings

One very important aspect to be addressed is the fact that fewer people feel the need to save their hard-earned cash these days. They will go as far as pretending that their expenses are too high to have the luxury of saving even a small portion of it. That's a mistake, no matter how much money you make.

REASONS: For some people saving a portion of their income every month might prove challenging. But, in general, people just don't feel like saving and it's due to various reasons:

- The lack of patience that saving in the long run may impose on you. People may have a hard time seeing the bigger picture, which is to have more buying power in the future (it could allow you to afford a new car, a down payment for a house, etc.), and also the self-discipline that emerges once you succeed in saving money for so long (meaning you are less tempted to touch your savings because you make more responsible spending decisions in your everyday life).

- The lack of understanding that saving money doesn't mean depriving yourself in the present. Actually, you should decide on a percentage that doesn't affect your present quality of life. For example, you could decide to save as low as $20 every month for the next six years, or $1,000 every month, depending on what you earn every month and on what you spend in terms of monthly obligations. Every little bit helps.

- The fact that most millennials prefer to be living for the moment and that everything around them seems to be influencing such behaviors (i.e., the attention, comparison, and validation from posting their lives on social media). A recent survey by LendEDU (done on 1,000 millennials) found that about 49% of millennials spent more on dining out per month than they put toward retirement. *(Instagram foodie, anybody?)* And strangely enough, 27% spend more on just coffee alone!

BENCHMARK: The principle behind saving is simple. Just like we said earlier, pick a percentage that will not penalize you when it comes to your monthly obligations and also take into consideration the amount you earn (being that you must be realistic when you decide to save money). But before you do this, you must know why saving is important:

- In the long run, it can help you focus on bigger goals (like buying a house or any big purchases).

- In the short run, it can help you take care of unexpected expenses without any outside help (like taking out loans to cover an emergency).

- It can also help you prepare for retirement and create wealth for the future (like accomplishing something after years of hard work).

After you've finally realized how important saving money is, you can now decide on how much you want to save every month. Let's look at one scenario with two different possibilities:

A person earns $1,500 per month. Their rent is $600, the utilities cost $50, food is $100, transportation $20, and for other items (like clothing or leisure), they spend $100 every month. So, their monthly obligation is $870, and they are then left with $1,500 - $870 = $630. Now, out of that $630, they can decide to take out between 10%, 15%, 20%, or 25% maximum (not more), according to how they manage their expenses. If they know that after totaling up their monthly obligation, they almost never run into any emergencies they can do the following: save up 25% of $630 every month, which is $157.50 every month, and keep the rest for unexpected expenses during the month (because you never know what may happen). If, on the other hand, they have a hard time minimizing unexpected expenses because, let's say, they have a loved one who needs financial assistance from time to time, they can choose to only save 10% of $630 every month, which is $63.

Now, in the long term by saving 25% of their remaining income after paying their monthly obligations, they will save $157.50 x 12 months x 10 years = $18,900.

On the other hand, if they choose to save up 10% of their remaining income after paying their obligations, they will then save $63 x 12 months x 10 years = $7,560.

If these were your options, this is only 10 years after you've started spending. Imagine how much you can save in 40 years (on average because you usually end up earning more through the years) after you decide to save up part of your income. Simply multiply each sum to see how much it makes in the course of 40 years with the same rhythm and you will find that for 25% of your earnings saved up, you save on average $75,600, and that with 10% of your earnings saved up, you save on average $30,240.

BENEFITS: The benefits here are endless because you end up not only accumulating some wealth but by not spending a portion of your earnings immediately, you also learn how to develop some kind of self-control when it comes to spending.

TASK: Work on your saving priorities by first figuring out your primary monthly expenses. After that, decide on what percentage you will pick (10%, 15%, 20%, or 25%) and decide on how much you wish to save every month from now on. Evaluate how much you will be able to save in 10 years, then evaluate how much this system can help you save for 40 years.

MISTAKE #3:
Using Traditional Banks Instead of Online Banks

In regard to savings, this may sound crazy but traditional brick-and-mortar banks seem to have fewer advantages than their online counterparts, and it can be costly for those folks who are barely earning enough to keep their accounts without having to pay any sort of maintenance fee because they can't always maintain a certain amount in their account.

REASONS: The interest rates are pathetically low for savings accounts opened at traditional banks (ranging between 0.05% to 1% for most banks); therefore, you don't really see any progress in your money, even after a long period of time. Added to this, it can be nerve-wracking to manage your monthly bills and at the same time keep a minimum balance in your account to avoid fees, which can be arduous if you have urgent expenses, thus restricting you in terms of withdrawal freedom.

BENCHMARK: Try opening accounts (savings or checking) with non-mainstream online banks. Why? Well, when compared to traditional banks, which already pay low interest rates and charge high fees every time you don't meet specific requirements, here are the main perks of online banks:

- Most online banks—for example, Ally Bank (ally.com), Synchrony Bank (synchronybank.com), CIT Bank (cit.com), PurePoint (purepoint.com), American Express Bank (americanexpress.com/personalsavings), and Discover Bank (discover.com/online-banking)— have no minimum balance requirement and no maintenance fees, while the popular big players like

Chase, Bank of America, HSBC, Citibank, and Wells Fargo do.

- The most attractive feature of these banks is the possibility to earn on average a 2-3% APY on your savings account (which might encourage you to save more, since you see your efforts to save help your money grow). The reason they can afford to offer higher interest is because of the lower operational costs from not having branch locations and staffs and lower marketing costs since fewer people hear about them.

- On another side note, online banks do give faster loan approval than traditional banks. Need a fast loan on a house about to be taken off the market? Online banks may be your calling card.

Despite all these advantages, some people still remain hesitant about using online banks due to their lack of existing branches, which is understandable for the convenience of completing transactions with a teller. However, online banks also provide many traditional services like wire transfers, digital check deposits (which traditional banks offer through their online applications), money transfer between accounts, bill payments, sophisticated security encryption, and, most important of all, FDIC insurance (to protect your money up to $250,000 just like any other banks). Just ensure that the bank is listed with the Federal Deposit Insurance Corporation (https://research.fdic.gov/bankfind) and not some fake bank.

The downside of online-only banks is the lack of ATMs for withdrawals, so you'll have to pay third-party ATM fees when you use one (although some online banks reimburse you for some ATM fees). So, if you plan to use ATMs frequently, you may not want to abandon traditional banks completely, but instead keep one traditional account open.

TASK: Look into opening an online bank account to help save for your future financial goals and objectives. Take note of the APY percentage you could earn after a period of time. Keep in mind that these rates do fluctuate depending on the Federal Reserve, so don't be surprised if your 3% eventually drops to 1.9%. In general, aside from some physical limitations, online banks are a monetary upgrade to brick-and-mortar banks.

MISTAKE #4:
Unnecessary Subscription Services Money-Eaters

Look around you—what do you see? *Subscription here. Subscription there. Subscription everywhere.* There always seems to be another ad to get you to sign up for another subscription because they're profitable for the companies that offer them.

Are you familiar with the *"get it for free by only paying shipping and handling, then you'll be enrolled in the monthly recurring plan"*?

Now, using a service because it's convenient and innovative is one thing. But using it excessively when unnecessary is another thing. In our society, everything is regulated by money, and those who succeed in it are the ones who are rational when it comes to their spending.

Getting to the main point—some people would rather spend money on services they don't need, especially subscription services. There are so many services that require recurring payments, and let's be fair, their prices are quite attractive. Take, for instance, the average monthly subscription for an online streaming service is between $10 to $13 a month, but then you also have monthly subscriptions for makeup items and clothing to add to your wardrobe starting at $10 a month.

REASONS: The real problem is that some of these subscriptions may sound tempting at first, but in reality, they serve no purpose in the long run other than to add to your physical or digital clutter and subtract from your bank account. Yes, we understand that sometimes you may want to watch a movie or that you might need wardrobe services from platforms that offer them. However, for items like designer perfumes, cosmetics, and even online television subscriptions, these services lose their usefulness after a while.

BENCHMARK: Here's what you should ask yourself when considering a subscription service:

- Will you really have time to use it, especially when it seems like you spend more time at work than at home.

- Will you really need the service in the long run? For example, if you're subscribed to Birchbox, which sends you cosmetics monthly for $10, would you need that many products every month, knowing that a bottle of body lotion can last for three months or more, and lipstick can last about nine months?

- Is it really necessary to have multiple streaming services, such as Netflix, Amazon Prime, and Hulu?

Yes, there are some shows and movies you can only watch on one service or the other. But why not pick the one that better suits your preferences overall? For example, pick the one service that you would likely spend more time watching, and then you should cancel the other one.

- Do you really need a subscription for certain services? Let's be honest, unless you are very bad at finding a good outfit in order to look chic, having outfits sent to your mailbox or doorstep every month is not mandatory. Instead, you can simply walk into any store and buy some clothing when you need it. The same goes for cosmetics. Just order them online as a one-time purchase, or simply go inside a store to get it yourself.

BENEFITS: By asking the right questions before succumbing to the temptation that comes with all these services being thrown at you, you get to pick what's more suited for you in terms of satisfaction (in the short or long term), and you also end up saving money every month and perhaps re-directing this money toward something more important, such as an emergency fund.

Let's look at an example. Imagine that your monthly budget in subscriptions alone included the following expenses:

- Netflix Premium Plan for $13.99/month, because that's what most people subscribe to, and you can also watch it on all your digital devices.

- Amazon Prime Video for $8.99/month, because you have access to more shows and movies.

- A Birchbox subscription for $13/month for cosmetics like skincare, hair care, nail products, and makeup. You get five products in a box every month. All products come in sample sizes (which is approximately 30 milliliters).

- A Stitch Fix shipping fee for new wardrobe items, which cost $20 per month for a five-piece outfit consistent with your lifestyle and taste. They also charge you for the outfits you keep, added on top of the $20 monthly shipping fee.

- A Dollar Shave Club subscription starting at $3/monthly for razor blades being mailed to you.

In total, you spend ($13.99 + $8.99 + $13 + $20 + $3) = $58.98 every month, which is ($58.98 x 12 months) = $707.76 per year.

The question is, do you really need all these services? If you were budget-conscious before getting all these subscriptions, you would have asked yourself:

- If you'll have the time to really use all these services.

- If these services are necessary for the long run.

- If there are any advantages for you to keep all these services.

- If certain services really need a subscription.

Now, go through your list of subscriptions covering all the pros and cons that emerge after asking these four questions, and you might end up with the following plausible solutions:

- Keep Amazon Prime Video as a way to watch movies and shows because it's cheaper, and it also gives you access to other networks (for instance, you can watch Game of Thrones on Amazon Prime Video where you can't on Netflix). So, you'll now pay $8.99 per month for online TV.

- It turns out that Birchbox was a waste of money, because not only will you end up paying for stuff you won't necessarily use in the end (too many products), but when you do the calculation you pay

$13 a month for five products that are 30 milliliters, which amounts to $156 a year only for cosmetics. With $30, however, on your own you can get one 100-milliliter lotion, one 100-milliliter shower gel, one lipstick, a 100-milliliter bottle of foundation that would last you much longer. And for you to spend $30 again to replace these products, you'll probably wait three to six months resulting in an annual spending between $120 ($30 x 4 quarters a year) or $60 ($30 x 2 times a year). By getting rid of unnecessary subscriptions like monthly cosmetic subscriptions, you'll save between $36 ($156 Birchbox - $120 DIY) and $96 ($156 Birchbox - $60 DIY).

- You decide to keep Stitch Fix, because not only are you satisfied with their services (thanks to them, you look good and are now great at matching colors), but you also never have the time to shop because you'd rather sleep during weekends in order to recover from your hard days at work. The fact that they do charge you money for clothing yet credit the shipping fees according to the value of what you decide to keep (after they send you your clothes), you don't really see the difference from when you go shopping for clothes. Plus, there are no subscription fees, just a styling fee every month for every time you need new clothing items. So, you're okay with the $20 styling fee per month.

- Another subscription is the Dollar Shave Club. Although it's relatively cheap, it won't really make any difference if you get a bunch of these products piling up that you won't necessarily get around to using, versus paying around $5-10 for a pack of normal razors that can last longer without the pressure of having to finish using them. You get money-saving flexibility over money-wasting convenience.

After reviewing your list of subscriptions (and making a few cancellations), you'll end up paying ($8.99 Amazon Prime

Video + $20 Stitch Fix styling fee) x 12 months = $347.88 added to your revised personal expenses that don't need a subscription—like $60 a year for cosmetics and $12 for razor blades—which gives you a personal expense total of $347.88 + $60 + $12 = $419.88. Subtract this $419.88 from the earlier amount that still contained these now-canceled subscriptions: $707.76. In the end, you save $287.88 a year.

TASK: Review all of the subscriptions and other expenses that are perhaps deemed unnecessary and cost you dearly each year. Get rid of subscriptions for services that are similar (i.e., if you have two or three streaming services, just keep one). For those that are really not necessary but costly in the long run, calculate how much it would cost to buy certain products directly at the store against having the same products being automatically ordered at a monthly fee).

MISTAKE #5:
Living Beyond Means

Another thing to think about is the fact that many people want to acquire nice fancy, expensive "stuff" when they know they don't make enough money. Most would say that it's because they don't set up plans or they simply want to forgo the unnecessary habits of older generations (baby boomers or the ones before them), who tried to avoid living beyond their means at all cost, since the standard of living has gone up.

This is something that many millennials would rather ignore today as their impulsive tendency to buy whatever they want seems to have reached beyond proportions.

REASONS: There's no real problem with wanting to buy a bike as long as you can afford it and also as long as you can live decently until your next payday. But that's not how young adults are thinking these days. Instead, they would rather buy the most expensive designer bag, "blow" their money on a motorcycle, and then move back in with mom and dad until they get back on their feet. This irresponsible spending is more frequent as spending priorities seem to have changed with this new generation.

According to a SmartAsset study, this generation would spend more on experiences compared to boomers. For instance, 40% of millennials have tattoos (which can cost between $100 and $300 per hour) or have had a body enhancement procedure. They also spend more on the latest technologies, like smartphones and tablets, which can cost between $900 to $1,500, and also on online luxury items (that can cost between $900 to $2,000 and more). It is clear that with all these great options, someone can easily end up living beyond their means very quickly.

BENCHMARK: What you should do is value the best opportunities you have compared to another opportunity you may have at the moment but which risks absorbing 80% of your income at once. What you should do is always stick with the opportunities that seem more reasonable when it comes to spending your money.

Let's explain: Imagine that you've just earned $3,000 after a hard month of working as security at a government building. You then randomly decide you want to spend at least $2,000 on a trip to Las Vegas. In your mind, you think that you might get lucky in Vegas and double or triple the money. But that's not likely because according to a *Wall Street Journal* report—on average, 11% of light gamblers end up winning, while only 5% of heavy gamblers end up winning. The possibility of you being one of those lucky winners is slim when you think about it. So, instead of taking the chance, do the following:

- Weigh your opportunities by first accounting for your obligations (rent + food + utilities for the month). Let's say your rent is $700 a month, your utilities cost you $80 a month, and you normally spend $150 a month on groceries with a total of $930, which leaves you with $2,070.

- Weigh the opportunity for an impulsive desire (such as going to Las Vegas for the weekend to gamble with $2,000) versus what that $2,000 can help you achieve in a more productive way. In this case, you have the opportunity to blow $2,000 at the casino and come back home with nothing *versus* picking three other options that are more beneficial. The three opportunities could be saving 25% of the $2,000, taking up leisure or a date to dinner and a movie (which could cost you at most $200), and buying some affordable furniture for your apartment (which could amount to $800).

BENEFITS: In the end, instead of blowing $2,000, you end up spending some of it on furniture for $800, saving $500, and only spending $200 on leisure. You can save the rest ($500) for emergency funds during the month. Overall, you are not only saving money but also spending it on useful stuff instead of losing it and risking moving in with relatives until you get back on your feet again.

TASK: Practice finding a true purpose behind your earnings by weighing some of your biggest current financial impulses (what you wish to spend most of your income on next, even though the money could be more useful on something else) and compare it to three other opportunities to spend that could be more beneficial in the short or long term. For example, instead of buying an $800 Louis Vuitton bag, you could divide the $800 in three smarter ways, allowing you to spend $200 on French classes, $300 for savings, and $300 on new sheets and other house supplies.

MISTAKE #6:
Not Budgeting Expenses to Avoid Accumulated Bills, Debts and Late Fees

To prevent yourself from ever digging into deep debt, you must set a number of financial spending priorities. When talking about financial priorities, people might see a very complex system with convoluted terms and calculations. But it doesn't have to be so complicated. When we talk about financial priorities, we are addressing the core of what it means to be "financially responsible."

Unfortunately, most of the problems encountered by millennials these days have to do with a lack of control over money or not knowing the true purpose of money. For example, the unrelenting love for Uber and Lyft over public transportation or walking for getting from one place to another, regardless of how short a distance, is burning major holes in every wallet; imagine paying $50 daily for commuting when a $2 bus fare would do just fine. As a result, many may not have enough money to timely pay important bills (like the phone bill, student loan repayment, or car payments). This may lead to the habit of having to pay more than they should (by being charged late fees for certain services), and other times, needing payment plans with incurred interest. Not to mention, the negative impact it has on their credit score.

REASONS: We live in an era where people seem to love pointing fingers when things go bad just to save face. Nobody wants to admit that they are wrong but instead, would blame others and then expect them to still assist them (like biting the hand that feeds you). The hard pill to swallow: We were told so many times that we could magically be whoever we wanted to be, *without* necessarily looking at the small steps needed to be taken in order to reach a goal. Thus, we've become negligent when it comes to being responsible with planning our financial lives. As mentioned earlier, millennials tend to favor experience rather than needs (with most of their budgets going to things like experience, luxuries, technologies, etc.); hence, they live more in the moment than thinking about the future.

BENCHMARK: Make a list of your immediate expenses (like rent, car payment, utilities, food, etc.). Then make a note of your short-term goals (like an immediate need that won't cost you too much and that you need to accomplish right away or during the course of this week/month). Next, mark down your long-term goals or non-immediate needs (like all the things that you need to do in six months to a year or longer, and which ones necessitate setting some money aside). After you create and label these lists, rank them from immediate financial priorities, mildly important financial priorities, and non-immediate financial priorities.

<u>BENEFITS</u>: Doing this allows you to immediately prioritize your urgent financial needs—with the choice to take care of your mildly important financial priorities—and ignore the less important ones for a later date, or at least until you are done taking care of your short-term goals (which are the mildly important financial priorities).

Let's explain with a scenario: Imagine that added to your rent, food, car, and utility expenses, you also wish to go to the gym this month to start your six-month weight-loss plan for a film shoot that will happen 12 months from now. You also wish to upgrade your car and get a BMW instead of a Toyota, but you don't want to fully finance the car; instead, you want to see how much you can put down to buy the car before getting a car loan. These are considered very important for you, and you know that you'll be making sacrifices concerning your lifestyle (regarding rent money, money for utilities, and even food). Right now, you don't know if you'll have to move back in with your parents, apply for food assistance, or opt for taking the bus to work in order to save up for your car. It is obvious that you have no clue what your priorities are and how you should handle or work on them. This is what you should do:

1. Make three lists, with your immediate financial priorities, your mildly important financial priorities, and your less important financial priorities. So, list one should include rent, food, car expenses, and utilities. List two should be gym expenses for your weight loss plan, and list three should be your savings plan for your new BMW.

2. Now, whatever earnings you have this month should first cover all your immediate expenses (on list one).

3. With the remaining amount, you can decide whether you need to go to the gym right away and carry on with this new routine for the next six months and whether you can also start saving up a certain portion of your earnings for your new car. But before deciding on what you should save for a car, you should do the following:

- Make sure you'll have a steady income where you will be able to subtract the same amount over a certain period of the year(s).

- Make sure the amount you subtract doesn't paralyze you for the rest of the month/year (meaning that you'll have to make sure you have enough to cover emergencies, gas expenses, and all over living expenses that help you continue living decently).

To illustrate, if you earn $2,000 a month, and your rent costs $800, you spend $150 on food for the whole month, $50 on utilities, and $100 on your (existing) car payment, before deciding to do anything else, deduct these immediate financial priorities from your earnings (which is $2,000 earning - $1,100 priority = $900). Now, decide whether you can afford to go to the gym for the next six months (which is $20 membership x 6 months) *versus* extracting 10%, 15%, 20%, or 25% out of your earnings to save for the car without facing problems financing it.

The optimum way to prioritize here is to go ahead with the gym membership, which costs very little (that's why it can be considered a "mildly important financial priority") for the next six months. And then, by the seventh month, start extracting 10%, 15%, or 25% out of your income in order to save enough money for the next 12 months and be able to minimize the costs of borrowing money to buy a car (giving you $900 x 25% x 12 months = $5,616, which could represent the money you will be able to put down on your car payment).

<u>TASK</u>: Write a list of your immediate financial priorities, another list of your mildly important financial priorities, and then a list of financial priorities that are less important. Make sure you take into consideration the explanations we've given as to why we label them this way.

MISTAKE #7:
Chasing Trends

Since when is having the latest trend in shoes, outfits, makeup, and even lifestyle a part of a monthly budget?

To the reasonable folks, this might sound like a random rhetorical question because they can gracefully come down from their materialistic high horses, once they glance at their current monthly bills and see that they are heading close to financial disaster territory.

For others, however, it is a way of life to constantly be chasing the next shiny objects because, again, priorities have evolved, and they are not the same as the generations' prior. Sadly, these priorities work against these victims of "shiny object syndrome."

REASONS: Part of the problem has to do with the role that new technologies and, consequently, platforms such as YouTube, Facebook, and Instagram have to play in the way we view the world, the way we see ourselves, and the way we aspire to live in our everyday lives. And it's not to undermine the benefits of these platforms (they can be educational and entertaining), but people spend too much time watching and listening to what some online "influencers" have to say and what they spend their money on.

Take a YouTube makeup artist who uploads content every week, and she recommends one new product per video. When some people watch, they see a glamorous and confident person wearing four different brands of makeup costing between $150 and $200 per product range. Then they will tell themselves that in order to look as glamorous and self-confident as this influencer, they too will have to buy the four products every time, which could end up costing between $600 and $800 per month, for makeup only.

BENCHMARK: Don't fall into all the artificial hype that comes from what's new and cool. Approach these platforms with a good head on your shoulders. Allow yourself to downgrade your options and acquire the same types of products but at a far more economical price, whether it's a luxury car, a high-fashion look, or celebrity-inspired cosmetics, etc. Some examples include the following:

- If you've always wanted to buy a BMW but ended up buying a Peugeot that almost looks the same and that you could afford, it's still okay. That's because although you may not have access to the same quality and the same options, they still look almost the same from the outside. So to preserve the bluff, take care of it as if it were a BMW (wash it, get its oil changed regularly, etc.). Take care of your possessions, and maybe you will see the real beauty in them.

- If brown Louis Vuitton bags are the trend this year but you can't afford one, it's okay. You can achieve the same look by getting a cheaper alternative like a brown Michael Kors bag. Choose the one look, color, shape, or custom that fits you or that you like the most because if you were inspired by a trend, people will not care that it isn't exactly the same as advertised.

- If the cosmetic product is advertised at Sephora, don't hesitate to look for the cheaper version in places like Walmart. Nobody said that you couldn't look good by being cheap; it's not so much about makeup but how you apply it. Always look for places that sell the same (or similar) product but at a bargain price. If spending $70 on makeup for the month will not affect the rest of your spending (meaning not sacrificing the money to pay for rent, water, food, etc.), then you are okay. Choose a look that you feel is affordable to your fixed budget that won't affect your other monthly responsibilities.

BENEFITS: You definitely save money here by downgrading your options. An everyday person who has obligations cannot keep up with all the advertisements or with the lifestyle that most influencers push on you by their sponsors. At the end of the day, it costs money, and only a small number of people can spend that much (considering that millennials only make up 13% of the wealth affluent market, according to SmartAsset).

TASK: From now on, have fun looking for alternatives to some of the trends. Pick a number of styles or products that you wish to own one day, and try to find their cheaper counterparts in bargain outlets like Walmart, Marshalls, and even Dollar Tree. You will see that you save more by being resourceful while staying in trend.

MISTAKE #8:
Not Favoring Frugal Minimalism

People, especially the younger generations, nowadays don't seem to realize that being financially well-off is not purely for show(ing off on social media). It is mostly so that you avoid ending up homeless and incapable of providing for yourself or your family. That's the whole point of all this.

But, what do we typically see happen when most people fall into financial distress or need to decrease their spending frequency or habit? They would rather borrow money and accumulate debt than endure the consequences of their actions or the hardship to get out of their predicament.

According to CNBC, one out of ten millennials (ages 23 to 38) has credit card debt for over five years, and one-fourth of all millennials carry credit card debt for at least a year—which is quite an alarming figure for such a small period of time.

<u>REASONS</u>: Our desires have gotten a lot more superficial, and technology and modernism may have a lot to do with it. All of this comes with the fact that we live in a consumer-driven society where we always want more, even the stuff we don't need. This leads to more money being wasted.

<u>BENCHMARK</u>: When times are hard and you need to turn your financial situation around, why not go frugal for a certain period of time? Going frugal may seem unattractive, but it carries with it a multitude of advantages:

- It helps you save money.

- It helps you reach goals.

- It helps you refine budgets.

- It helps you locate money mistakes.

- It helps you appreciate the little things.

- It helps you get a fresh start at the end.

These are just some of the things adopting a frugal life of minimalism can help you achieve. Do the following when going from materialistic to minimalistic:

1. Make an extensive list of all the things you believe you overspend on—it could be that you buy too many snacks, that you buy clothing every month which is also excessive, etc. Evaluate this list in terms of how much you spend on these items monthly, then delete them from your shopping list. By deleting them from your shopping list or diminishing the frequency at which you buy them, you actually know how much you'll be saving for a month.

2. Make a list of the things you truly need—like staying current on your car payment, paying the IRS some IOU money, saving money for your kid's next school year, etc. Just write a list of whatever you feel is always left out but that you truly need. In other words, things you know that most of your money should go to. Evaluate this list to know how much money you will need to at least take care of 90% of them, or make a payment plan that you will be able to honor and not end up being penalized. Therefore, the amount you will come up with will become your goal to reach.

3. Decide on the duration of your new frugal lifestyle. Are you going into it for six months, nine months, or ten months? Remember this will help you reach a goal and also help you get back on track financially.

4. Make sure you take note of all the additional adjustments you will need in order to make this new phase of your life a success. For instance, think about

the additional hours of work you will have to do, and all the cost-effective stuff you will have to buy instead as well as a limitation on the number of those items to buy. So, when you set up your new adjustments, remember that it is about downgrading your choices, quantities, and, perhaps, quality—like if you used to shop at Sephora for cosmetics, going to Dollar Tree for a few cheaper items won't hurt.

- Additionally, one thing that most people seem to omit these days is the use of coupons. *Recall the nostalgic old days when grandma would cut out orange juice coupons from grandpa's Sunday paper?* Well, coupons still exist. They are not difficult to find because your mailman delivers most of them to your mail on a regular basis, or you can find them in newspapers or simply go online to gain wider coupon access to more goods (the ones you will really need when adopting this new lifestyle). Most stores even have customer loyalty reward programs that earn you points for the amount you spend to be redeemed as savings. Just walk in, inquire about them, and sign up.

BENEFITS: You will value money a bit more and learn a lesson or two about money management—in the sense that it shouldn't be a fancy concept or something formal for someone who went to business school but, instead, something that can help you prosper and see things for what they truly worth and the struggles as just phases that can be overcome.

TASK: Follow our guidelines on what it takes to start having a more frugal lifestyle. Remember to downgrade some of your choices by going economical and buying only what you need. So, if you liked buying 10 boxes of Lays chips every month, you could reduce this to one. And also don't forget to erase whatever is unnecessary from your buying list.

MISTAKE #9:
Instant Gratification Upbringing Culture

Today, the majority of people (from ages 20 to 38) think that having a job means that you can overnight ask for a property loan, drive a dream car, or instantly start going away on fancy vacations—or even start taking care of their parents. This is a big money mistake because, in the long run, you might end up losing everything.

REASONS: Many have lost sight of what a life cycle is, especially when it comes to adulthood and how things should be handled financially when you reach that period of your life. It may be attributed to the abandonment of basic useful knowledge that was once passed down from one generation to another. This practice has become antiquated with the advancement of so many faster options and automated solutions.

This could explain why people are so used to having things done for them and become impatient when they don't get their way, now! *You have a problem?* Better call someone to fix it. *You're hungry?* GrubHub is your new best friend. *You want to go somewhere?* Don't worry, Uber will be there in five minutes. Do you see the correlation here? There's a digital solution for everything just a few clicks away straight from your phone. This attitude of instant automation does not prepare people for the realities that await them (which is to work hard to achieve your dreams). As a result, people often end up burned out and hopeless after 10 years of believing that they could automatically be whoever they want—without thinking of what it takes to be that person.

BENCHMARK: Cut out a bunch of small pieces of paper and get three baskets (or any jar or container). On each piece of paper, write all the things you have done or want to do in order to become the ideal person. Put them into one basket and label it, "me." Label the other baskets "discard" and "keep." Now, knowing you've been wanting to achieve all these things now (meaning in a year or less), think about all the things that are too unrealistic to achieve because you simply don't have enough time or money. Move those things to the discard basket. For all the things that you were able to achieve successfully, put them in the keep basket. You will probably see that the items in the discard basket outnumber the ones in the keep basket, and that's because your expectations are too high and that you want everything right away.

BENEFITS: You can easily avoid being choked by your bad financial choices or financial performance. Perhaps you can take more time to become this successful person you've always wanted to be by taking advantage of all the time you still have, and think about changing certain ways of how you do things. Remember that you are not perfect and it is because you are not perfect that you are able to learn and rectify yourself.

<u>TASK</u>: Use this basket method to put all the things you wish to accomplish immediately in the "me" basket—then, polish that "me" and make your dream more achievable by putting the unrealistic hopes in the "discard" basket and the more attainable ones in the "keep" basket.

MISTAKE #10:
Overreliance on Social Programs for Financial Assistance

On the surface, receiving assistance from the government seems like a great idea to help pay for your bills and food without you having to work so hard to provide for yourself. After all, who doesn't love free stuff? But it's a huge trap you don't want to fall into.

Government aids are primarily designed to help people with temporary needs, not a permanent solution. The longer you stay in them, the harder it is to crawl out of that hole you're in because the deepening effect is further conditioning you to be dependent upon them. And what happens when the government suddenly decides to cut some of its programs that you rely on—not to mention the deficit that the U.S. has been in what seems like forever, so don't be surprised if they do.

<u>REASONS</u>: Government assistance in the form of food stamps, vouchers for preschoolers, WIC programs for young children, and housing assistance can make people lazier, which results in them lacking discipline over their expenses when the government is always there to have their back. For the millennials who are interested in welfare benefits, the fact is that they are more attracted by socialism—without even knowing what it means or who would finance such a system, according to Brad Polumbo when he was editor for the non-profit organization Young Voices.

Although some people don't have the choice and deserve these benefits (like people with disabilities who can't work), there are many causes for such behavior, including:

- People who were born into a poor family who used to benefit from these types of programs and have figured out that by not reporting their change of income after living in low-income housing should give them additional years of minimum rental expenses.

- People who have a hard time taking responsibility for their own lives and refuse to improve themselves.

- People who would rather take minimum paying jobs just to maintain their condition and continue receiving their benefits.

People in these three categories believe that by "gaming the system," their monthly expenses are covered. In reality, these people aren't learning to make wise financial decisions in the long run because they are being "taken care of."

BENCHMARK: If you happen to be relying on government benefits and have your own dreams, inspire yourself to come out of this cycle by doing the following:

- Get yourself to work and determine how long you wish to receive these benefits (3, 6, 9, 12, 18 months?)

- Improve your relationship with money by avoiding the same mistakes that you used to make and led you down this path (no financial planning, no financial discipline, unnecessary spending habits, etc.).

- Go back to school or get some professional training to increase your chance at earning better paychecks.

BENEFITS: Instead of hiding from your responsibilities, you get to think outside the box and take all the opportunities that come your way. And remember that the more chances you take, the more you get what you want in life.

TASK: Change the course of your life now. Regain your self-confidence and pride by leaving these government benefits to those who really need them and become wiser with the way you spend your money.

MISTAKE #11:
Oblivion to Health Insurance

Dealing with monthly bills *linked* to a health insurer might feel like a rip-off, because let's face it, most people would prefer to pay for a hospital bill only when they visit the doctor for a serious illness, than paying for a monthly bill that might not be necessary. Plus, a 2016 Harris Poll showed that one in five adults aged 18 to 36 claimed they couldn't afford health care costs to begin with. Although this way of thinking might make economic sense for most of us, there's a huge problematic risk factor involved.

REASONS: The problem lies with the fact that you never know what type of health emergency you may come across one day (for example: cancer, a serious car accident, etc.).

Once the health emergency has hit you, you may not be ready at all because hospital bills tend to be astronomically high (which may lead to more debt accumulation in the end).

BENCHMARK: It's quite simple. Just get familiar with your health insurance options at the beginning of the year. Take note of things you need to know firsthand:

- You will pay a monthly premium based on the category of your plan.

- There are four metal categories to pick: bronze, silver, gold, and platinum. They each determine how you and your plan split the costs of your health care (they have nothing to do with the quality of care). Take, for instance, the bronze category, your insurer pays 60% of the bill, while you pay 40%. For the platinum category, which is the most expensive premium but your insurer pays 90% of the bill, you only pay 10%.

- Premiums for individuals are cheaper than the ones paid by families. An individual can pay on average a $321 premium, while a family premium can go up to $833 per month.

- Health insurance plans use clinics or doctors that are a part of their network. So, you may not have access to certain doctors or health facilities depending on the network your insurance covers.

- You may be charged a co-pay amount every time you visit the doctor, which amounts to the percentage not covered by your insurer (which ranges as high as 40% and as low as 10%, depending on the metal category of your plan).

- You must also take into account factors like age, location, tobacco usage, and the number of people insured, which all determine the final cost of your plan. For example, when it comes to age, sometimes the older you get, the more you end up paying for health insurance.

Depending on your needs, the total cost of your plan depends on what you want covered. This means besides regular visits to a medical doctor or dedicated health specialist, you may add a dental and vision plan to it, which may cost more.

BENEFITS: Despite getting billed monthly, having health insurance can help you prevent certain diseases and detect or address certain health issues that you may have been oblivious to, and it also helps you avoid some high hospital bills (like after the birth of a child). Remember, health is true wealth.

TASK: Take your time to explore the different health insurance companies. Make sure you inquire about the different plans available, what the health plans covered (seeing what you can afford each month is also crucial), and, also, if you'll have access to any health facilities you wish to go to or if your plan only allows you a restricted list of doctors.

MISTAKE #12:
Not Investing and Planning for Retirement Now

Here's an important one, so pay attention.

First of all, there's nothing wrong with keeping some of your hard-earned cash at home. It can come in handy for any rainy day or sudden emergency. Yet, monetarily speaking, there's an underlying drawback with this method of storing your money for the future at home (and even, surprisingly, with saving your money in the bank).

<u>REASONS</u>: The hidden problem comes from the ever-increasing inflation of the dollar—that devaluates the buying power of it. One way to help offset that is by

putting your money in online banks savings accounts with higher interest rates.

For example, if you have saved $500 by the end of every year for a 10-year period (which will accumulate to a total of $5,000 by the tenth year), it will not have the same effective value if you were saving the same amount for 10 years with an online bank that offers 2.10% yearly interest rate (which would amount to around $6,168.35 by the tenth year). The 2.10% sounds decent enough since most brick-and-mortar banks can't even go above 0.05%.

However, this won't entirely beat inflation. You NEED to be investing now and planning for your retirement as early as possible.

BENCHMARK: Think about investing in an investment account—preferably a retirement account like an IRA or Roth IRA that has tax benefits—where your money will eventually receive all the adjustments needed and maintain its true value even 10 years later.

Investing is honestly not as difficult as it may seem nor as scary as the media tries to put it. Yes, there is always risk in any investment; however, we're going for the safer route in investing for the long term—not the trying-to-get-rich-overnight or short-term day trading—meaning you put money in an account and leave it there to grow for decades.

What should you invest in? Most people think about popular companies like Facebook and Apple, but then again, there could always be another Facebook and Apple later down the road. *(The next WeChat, maybe?)*

To reiterate, we're going for the safer long-term approach, so the recommended route is to invest in "fund stocks" that comprise of multiple companies or a sector, rather than "individual company stocks." Why? Because new companies can come and go, but the funds you invested in can substitute those defunct companies with the next big things. Do note here that the potential reward may not be as great due to the lower risk, contrasted with if you have accidentally gotten in early with the next unknown Amazon company in its infancy. Nevertheless, you can rest easy and sleep better at night by not stressing out whether that riskier company is going through turmoil.

The best fund to get started is the "S&P 500 Index Fund" because it is made up of the top 500 companies in the United States and that list is updated regularly whenever new companies make the list. Plus, the S&P 500 has been around for almost a century. Even investment tycoon Warren Buffett says: "Put 10% of the cash in short-term government bonds and 90% in a very low-cost S&P 500 index fund."

<u>BENEFITS</u>: The importance of keeping up with the inflation of the dollar is indisputable for reasons like:

- Having the money you've made through your investment will allow you to accomplish things you want to do during retirement. After all, retiring doesn't mean life has to be stagnant.

- Being able to still live comfortably in the future. The appreciated amount of money in your account becomes automatically adjusted for inflation to match the higher cost of living.

TASK: Start investing! You can have this managed by a broker or do it all by yourself.

- If you prefer having a broker—stop by investment firms like Charles Schwab, Merrill Lynch, Morgan Stanley, and TD Ameritrade. This is great if you want somebody there guiding you along the way, but the downside, of course, is typically the fees.

- If you prefer doing it yourself—you can do so at home with services like Robinhood (robinhood.com), Acorns (acorns.com), Betterment (betterment.com), Wealthfront (wealthfront.com), and M1 Finance (m1finance.com). Thanks to modern technologies, investing is no longer reserved for the financially savvy but also for the everyday individual, who can easily get started by filling out simple questions then receiving a customized approach that suits their investment goal. The best part is most of these are free or have low fees to use. But the tradeoff is that you will hardly get any assistance, and there's very little human interaction when you need it. Look into them and consider all your options.

DISCLAIMER: This is not official investment advice, so take all that we are saying here with a grain of salt and always consult with a professional financial advisor.

MISTAKE #13:
Lack of Good Overall Personal Financial Plan

If you thought that financial plans were only necessary for businesses or big corporations—think again. Everyone can benefit from having a financial plan, just on a smaller scale. Think about it. The term "financial plan" literally means a program or schedule for how to handle your finances at a given period of time.

Now, don't you have to make financial decisions almost every day in order for you to survive? It takes money to do so, right? Overall, people need to plan what they will do with their money in the short, medium, and sometimes, long term.

<u>REASONS</u>: People don't seem to want to bother doing all this stuff and would rather opt for the easy or lazy route. Take for example, it is far easier to borrow money than having to look at the more functional way of dealing with things, so many people would rather get a loan and be in debt than take the time to come up with a personal financial plan. To truly evaluate your money, you need to look at your personal needs and wants in a short or long period of time. And after allocating these values, you should then look for ways or means to come up with the money (through savings or reduced spending) and spend the money (by carefully selecting which expense should come first).

<u>BENCHMARK</u>: It is not difficult. Just follow these steps:

1. Write down all your personal needs and wants (living expenses, leisure expenses, things you wish to afford one day, etc.).

2. Jot down the value of each item, for instance, living expenses = $1,000 per month, leisure expenses = $300, things you wish to afford in the short or long run amounting to $500 and sometimes $1,000 depending on the item.

3. List ways to cover your living expenses (such as working your regular job).

4. List ways to cover your leisure expenses (such as taking up additional side hustles).

5. List ways to cover the things you wish to acquire immediately or in the future (such as saving up some money for long-term items like a house, car, or new computer).

6. List clearly which item should be bought first, typically when it comes to things you wish to afford immediately or during the course of the year. For example: if you want to buy a house, a car, a luxury bag,

designer shoes, or jewelry. It is clear that jewelry will come first with a minimum estimated cost of $300; the designer bag will come second with an estimated minimum cost of $500; the car will come third, and probably after six to 12 months of savings, with a minimum down payment of $5,000; and the house with a minimum savings period of five years and $30,000 as a down payment would be last.

After setting up this portion of the plan, it should be about hard work, coming up with a realistic but good personal savings strategy and also making a few sacrifices (like downgrading your spending habits or going frugal).

BENEFITS: By using a financial plan, you are guaranteed not to waste money but use it wisely to end up getting what you want. Having a financial plan also gives you ideas on the type of personal discipline to adopt in order to reach your goals and simply live a decent life.

<u>TASK</u>: Set up your own personal financial plan by following the guidelines mentioned. (Write down all your personal needs and wants, write the value of each item then rank them from the most affordable to the least affordable, and write ways on how to cover each of these expenses).

ENCORE ACT:
A Self-Financial Planner Meeting

TASK 1: Make up a budget for your meals by opting to buy groceries instead of eating out. Apply these few principles: make a list, make a budget for the items on the list, learn the basics of cooking, then make eating at home more functional by learning how to preserve your meals for a whole week.

TASK 2: Work on your savings, by first writing down all your primary monthly expenses. After that, decide on what percentage you will pick (10%, 15%, 20%, or 25%) and decide on how much you wish to save every month from now on. Evaluate how much you will be able to save in 10 years, then evaluate how much this system can help you save for 40 years.

TASK 3: Consider exploring all the advantages that online banks provide to their customers by comparing things like the APY rate that your traditional bank offers you versus the ones that some online banks offer. List five more advantages that these banks offer compared to traditional banks, like more enthusiasm to save money, no fees or charges when the account is empty for a while, etc.

TASK 4: Use the basket method to put all the things you wish to accomplish now in the "me" basket. Then weed out that "me" basket and make your dream more realizable by moving your unrealistic hopes to the "discard" basket and the more attainable ones on the "keep" basket.

TASK 5: Make a list of your immediate financial priorities, another list of your mildly important financial priorities, and then a list of your least important financial priorities. Answer the following questions:

- Are you sure all your immediate priorities really belong to that category? Explain your answer.

- Do you think that less important priorities can be postponed to the following month? Explain why.

F(ULL) ACE AT REVEAL:
Patched-Up Deeper Pockets

Dealing with money is never easy because it's not only about making money and paying bills, but it's also about making the right financial decisions and moves that can help you become someone one day and live the way you've always wanted to.

Even though people seem to have a hard time understanding why it's often challenging for them to obtain some financial stability or something as simple as having just enough to live a decent life, learning to plan your expenses is the important first step. And while it may not entirely be a walk in the park, it doesn't have to be a sprint from a hungry lion either.

Adopting practical applications—like ranking financial priorities, downgrading your choices, embracing frugality, weighing opportunity costs, investing money for the long term, as well as taking the courage to work your way off the government dependency cycle—can really save you all the time and trouble in the world and really help you give value to your money.

Avoid the mistakes and carry out the best practices we provided to finally take control of your financial destiny today.

Financial Mistakes

Financial Mistakes

www.ingramcontent.com/pod-product-compliance
Lightning Source LLC
Chambersburg PA
CBHW070401220526
45467CB00001B/453